"In *Dear Animal,* as in the salutation to a frank and feisty love letter, the poet is a 'pure bird of the street,' a 'rock dove,' or maybe 'Joan of Arc,' and the poems are populated by animals of all descriptions, an imperfect, gendered zoology. It's the source of her boundless will and power. She tells us, 'See through me. See the violet of my natural disaster, my exposed boutique,' demonstrating her knowledge with intimate vignettes, vivid lists, tales of her yearnings and exploits. Her word play sparkles—fluttery butterflies tossed in the air— 'mandrake,' 'fetterbush,' 'fauve,' 'sword sheather,' 'Vitruvian.' 'Why all the tremble and janksy?' the poet asks. When there is the power of 'the giant eye, / the grand opening, / the place where you first appeared / hungry and glimmering—' She says, 'I'm a crime.' But if these gorgeous and graphic poems, full of devotion, read as criminal, sign me up for their poetic justice.'

– JOYCE JENKINS, editor-director of *Poetry Flash,*
director of Watershed Environmental Poetry Festival

DEAR ANIMAL,

NOMADIC PRESS

OAKLAND
111 FAIRMONT AVENUE
OAKLAND, CA 94611

BROOKLYN
475 KENT AVENUE #302
BROOKLYN, NY 11249

WWW.NOMADICPRESS.ORG

MASTHEAD
FOUNDING AND MANAGING EDITOR
J. K. FOWLER

ASSOCIATE EDITOR
MICHAELA MULLIN

DESIGN
BRITTA FITHIAN-ZURN

MISSION STATEMENT
Through publications, events, and active community participation, Nomadic Press collectively weaves together platforms for intentionally marginalized voices to take their rightful place within the world of the written and spoken word. Through our limited means, we are simply attempting to help right the centuries' old violence and silencing that should never have occurred in the first place and build alliances and community partnerships with others who share a collective vision for a future far better than today.

INVITATIONS
Nomadic Press wholeheartedly accepts invitations to read your work during our open reading period every year. To learn more or to extend an invitation, please visit: www.nomadicpress.org/invitations

DISTRIBUTION
Orders by teachers, libraries, trade bookstores, or wholesalers:

Small Press Distribution
1341 Seventh Street
Berkeley, California 94701
spd@spdbooks.org
(510) 524-1668 / (800) 869-7553

DEAR ANIMAL,

© 2016 by MK Chavez

This book was made possible by a loving community of chosen family and friends, old and new.

For author questions or to book a reading at your bookstore, university/school, or alternative establishment, please send an email to info@nomadicpress.org.

Cover Art by Larassa Kabel

Published by Nomadic Press, 111 Fairmount Avenue, Oakland, California 94611

Third printing, 2020

Library of Congress Cataloging-in-Publication Data

Dear Animal,
p. cm.

Summary: *Dear Animal,* is a re-imagination of the Linnaean taxonomy from a feminist perspective. This collection is a love letter to the resilient feral female and an exploration of the myriad Animalia that dwell in the margins.

[1. Women. 2. Poetry. 3. American General.] I. III. Title.

LIBRARY OF CONGRESS CONTROL NUMBER: 2016913221

ISBN 987-0-997-933-6-0

DEAR ANIMAL,

MK CHAVEZ

NOMADIC PRESS

for those who fight back
tooth and nail

Artemis

Come ride
my
ovarian horns.
Down
with the captive
Clitori.
Be free
&
speak
my
grizzly
bear
lips.

CONTENTS

AMPHIBIA: COLD AND GENERALLY NAKED

PISCES: VORACIOUS APPETITES

MAMMALIA: NATURAL ENEMY

INSECTA: SMALL ANIMALS OF SENSATION

AVES: FLIES IN THE AIR AND SINGS

VERMES: IMPERFECT ANIMALS

Convocation

I always knew that I would burn. I knew it even at eleven, standing in the Jehovah Hall wearing a Pepto-Bismol pink crinoline dress, my knobby knees rubbing the rough fabric, the itch of fabric and a forced smile. The force was upon me like damp fur. I could smell it, the danger of it, God, and the stink of anti-sinner. I was wearing a mask, a forced slash of a smile carved onto my face, a thick silk sash wrapped around the waist, it was falling, and unfurling. The banner of Jehovah hanging above everyone's head and a boy stood next to me, shiny, his hair greased slick, black as a seal, his eyes black diamonds, and his mouth red as fire. The banner expanded toward the crowd, pregnant with air, announcing *Doers of God's Word*, and then deflated, the letters pulling into themselves, skinny and severe, as if meeting the crowd was a disappointment. Around us a congregation of black flies buzzed in the heat, the infernal pitch, the repetitive dull pulse that set off the cochlear nerve, pushing against the tympanic membrane, a constant drone, *Run*, and *Tear off that dress*, it hummed, and that growing itch grew, as did the urge to scratch. The boy leaned into my ear. The buzz swirling around me and the heat emanating from his breath, volcanic, erupting into sound, *Let's go to the pool. Do you have a swimsuit?* And before I speak, he had fished the answer out of my eyes. *It's ok, we can swim naked*, he said. He swallowed my hand in his, sweaty and sticky, like I imagined the fly's legs might feel when they rub them together, recalling their last meal, considering the future of the eggs they've laid.

San Quentin Senryu

Building a prison

in a beautiful place

act of kindness, cruelty

The Rise and Fall of the Scorpion

He made the big exit through Hollywood's Chateau Marmont.

He was used to the young celebs—breaking
out was a shock.

This was a crazy place. People swore they could see him
do things. Have you?

He's not perfect. Did not clean the hotel room
before he checked out.

He was the first older guy to put a live scorpion
down my pants.

He wouldn't be snagged. Tried to cover his tracks
by setting up the usual spikes.

Hit a little trouble spot.
Gave a false sense of security.

He'll still be doing the hustle,
leaving crimson patches in the afterglow.

I'll cry often, thinking of him.

The Procession

I am writing to you because there has been a death.
I carried my wife's body from where it lay
covered in a fine layer of dust. Everything
about her, almost perfect:

>pleated skirt still
>pleated, blouse
>buttons buttoned, even
>her stockings remained.

The only sign of her departure was the small gathering
of nylon at her ankles, her legs and waist no longer
holding the tension that once kept the stockings
tight against her warm flesh. I cannot tell you
how she felt about the light layer of dust
that marred the perfect blackness of her skirt.

I cannot tell you how I felt. There were so many eyes
looking at us. I can tell you that the idea
of her upset the idea of me. I stopped walking
at one point and all the eyes stopped with us.
I could no longer tell who they were looking at,
and I could no longer tell which one of us has died.

I can tell you there is a photograph,
and I am there, and she is there, slack
in my arms. Behind us, so many eyes.
Beyond them, a wall of broken stones.

Observations in New Orleans

A Tennessee Williams quote
decorates a wall on Royal Street

Hell is yourself . . .

Neverending cities of the dead.
Bourbon Street, a dark-haired girl
in an off-white dress
rolling a crystal ball on the tips
of her fingers. A sea of tourists
swallows her whole.

Beads fly and men bark.

The hustle of brown-eyed
docile mules pulling buggies
on the historical tour.

Man playing guitar smiles, black teeth.

No fortune for the teller. Everyone knows.

Laugh and laugh, drink and drink.

Meat Tags

Tears are not the same in different countries.
        Not the same for you and me.
        My first boyfriend still lives
        in San Quentin which is a place
        unto its own. He'll die of Hep C,
        which is a terrain of pummeled meat.

The liver holds anger.
        You can build bruises
        from carrying something
        that weighs too much.

The petal skin of my inner thigh blossomed
        red & purple. I was
        perpetually sad
        that we had no future.

We didn't cry, and for different reasons.
        He can't be seen to have the weakness
        of a woman
        and I don't cry
        because it's dangerous
        to be woman.

In this foreign land
            we call home, a teardrop
            is tattooed at the corner of our eye
            to let the world know that you don't
            have to go far to fight a war.

My Little Pony

found poem, language from The Mustang Ranch's Erotic Menu

Consider this foreplay.
>Crossed out eyes,
>feed your desires,
>something to whet
>the appetite, a private
>parade of nighties, nylons,
>garters, and panties.

Fire & Ice
>Ladies sit still, as you like,
>Kama Sutra specialties.
>*De La Maison*
>pornographic
>fingertips. Too good to be
>a la carte twice as nice,
>French tease, holds liquid
>of different temperatures
>in the mouth. Titillates
>your bungalow.

Full pleasure
        for straight lay,
        wild tour, half &
        half, everyone performs.

This horse
        cuts through flesh,
        save room for a little
        for more. Please come
        to visit, friends await,
        you, the World
        Famous Mustang
        Ranch.

The Affair

Nocturnal like most vermin,
we feed on remnants
and on the soured breath
of our lives. We loll
suckling on flesh
primitive
and sinewy.
Likeness of one
another
and the world around us.

Baby Our Sorrow

after Mark Ryden's painting The Birth *1994*

Busy with the impending rue
you forgot to feed the knotted
bud. The only bulb that could emerge—
a weakened mandrake, not quite human,
retreated rightly into what it knew best.
Burrowed in the dirt, never to be seen again.

Ideation

Walk on the snail trail
past the coy and the failed.
Pick up snail by snail,
they mumble
from a mucus-covered membrane,
it's best not to coddle
the kind of sunshine
that comes from a bottle.
I think of Alice
popping pills.
Ache
for that orange glow,
the familiar cylinder, vacant smile.
Sit & wait bait,
quite alone
on the medicine shelf.
My head is a new exhibition,
jaws of old mold,
synaptic break crackle snap.
This is just one day in the park,
rain brain,
clean sink,
consider what's left,
gunk stuck,
the bottom
some sad
brain drain.

The Eighth House (The House of Sex)

The pink tongue of my desire
transpires to make new words
to describe our lips, which

together make conceptual art.
A fever dream that utters
nonsense, builds heat

in the small of my back.
Sleek tips of muscles touch,
create flesh psychedelia,

make my heart beam dayglow,
red pulsing heliotrope
in my throat.

The secret between your mouth

and mine, a revolver,

brazen fervor, blind boomerang.

The collision of our breath

makes the universe fall,

when your hands touch my face

everything opens, leaves

me a convoluted mess—

you give me this:

Autobiography # 2

The world is cold as salamanders. Meanwhile, a kiss comes along and there's a tremor in June. The lover says this pot is black is beautiful. Together, we remember how good it is to strut. We encircle the fauve. Come all to see our somewhat fractured and shiny reflection. Our sex is imbued with the politics of rosaries. When imagining us, see Eros the bittersweet. We surpass the unreachable, ricochet the connotation of the solitary red fruit. How a loaded mouth fingers the trigger. We are the secret urchin, this is our place in history. Despite it all, I like how we look. What a turn on. Let's not mind being the abomination. It could be fun to drink tea from a fur-lined cup.

What I Might Carry in the Small Cave of My Mouth

Malcontent forked my tongue.

It's a mystery spot.

How do you do that?

That was the first question.

And then the statement:

You've got a mouth on you.

I tie cherry stems.

My mouth is a shady place,

the very tool that served as proof—

it got the witches burned.

It has licked and licked. It's electric-tipped,

the animal you meet before the beast dentata.

The cave you lower yourself into because the risk is low,

or so you think.

AMPHIBIA: COLD AND GENERALLY NAKED

Disneyland

Cartoon rides & big sad eyes.
Mickey signs with his deformed
hands, *get out while you still can.*

The witch, a semi-employed actress
takes a polaroid with you and whispers
into your ear, don't go to sleep.

All heads nod.

Have you ever noticed
that Mickey has no balls?
says a man. Some husband
gnaws on a big fat bone
and yells at his wife,
Better shut your pie hole.

Candy apples, tacky taffy, and pink
sugar-cotton-coated fingertips.

That magical moment
when your body is propelled into the sky.

Silly clown, you're bound
to come down.

Oh Dumbo, this is not
the happiest place on earth.

The Melancholy of US Architecture

If you open the box
 you may find walls
  that end in sky
   Everything built
    now stands
     dilapidated
      in the rusted landscapes
       of deserts
      Open sand
     and it may lead
   to Ghana
 where water
 once broke stone
Open water and
 you may find
a flood of ships
 cotton
  indigo
   & quills

declarations

      emancipations

            & the lost

               forty acres

         & a mule

     taking

   their place

next to

the history of us.

A Sterling Elegy

Kareem Abdul Jabbar says, *There's light now.*
To define light, open a kaleidoscope of color.

Warm skin is optimistic. So alive.
This little light of mine. This little light of yours.

My friends says, *It's 2014 and it's like we're still
living on a plantation.* I am writing a poem

about addicts in Iran, because I cannot bear
the NPR coverage of addiction in another country,

because I cannot bear coverage of addiction
in this country. I pledge not to be discouraged

by news. When the news breaks about Sterling
I say I don't expect much from a man who owns

other men. There's not much new here. Yet,
I wait for the verdict because once I did not,

and look what happened. Light
can be a surprise, a shock,
a could you have imagined this is still
going on.

Voice Culture

Language is gut. Twisted rope.

To breathe is not a privilege.

Disruption is disturbance.

I'm sorry that I've disturbed your bagel I'm
sorry that I've disturbed your cream cheese I'm sorry
that I've disrupted your Americano, your silent
breakfast, your newspaper, your New York breakfast,
your civilization.

Excuse me, I'm dying—
but I can't be
stopped. I'm being.

I'm sorry that I've disturbed your smoked salmon I'm
gasping, asking.

I'm sorry that I've disrupted the tiny capers
& poppy & sesame seeds
with my living.
Excuse the disruption
of my being.

Disruption being and breathing.

Maybe we be rude. Rude instance,
insistence, maybe we be weeds, dandelions
powerful as lions heads.

I'm a crime. Disruption
direct from distortion.

With a Mouth Like That

This ain't
No pretty saint

Fruit of thy womb

Riff

No
please

Let me wash your dirty feet

No tears

No petal-lipped chick

I'm Shiva
I have a well-hung tongue

After I baby-kiss the bird of your brain
I'll steal your perfect teeth
String them like pearls

Bite you to bits
Bring you to the end

Your doll face floating in the sky
Between my fleshly
thighs

I'll

Hollow   you   out
My   lips   sticky
Like   sap   tapped
from a sugar tree

Hurry open up and let me see

How to Write a Love Letter

Dear

> I thought about you today. It was a day
> like any other day except that I saw a Komodo
> dragon eating a bunny. The dragon's smirk
> reminded me of you, and it made me think
> about your teeth, and the feel of cold enamel
> against the fleshy part of my thigh.

Dear

> I didn't think about you today.

Dear

> When I thought of you today, I thought of a nest
> of baby starlings, the translucent featherless
> flesh of their gullets stretched toward the sky
> begging to be fed.

Dear

Today is a milky gray day. The sky is bereft
of hope and I thought about how your body looked
stretched across the once clean sheets of my bed
after we'd had sex. I remember the sharpness
of your bones poking through flesh, jaw, elbow,
and kneecap, and how there was no softness to you
at all.

Dear

Last night I dreamt of you. I was trapped in a house
with a million rooms. You were behind each door.
It was the end of the world and I was trying
to save the children. I thought of you when I woke
alone in my bed, said your name out loud
and waited, smiling into the silence.

Industrial Vagina

Vagina is shark, is lockjaw.
Pit bull of my sexuality,
my sensuality.
No wonder—the awe.

And it has been said,

>   *That bitch is in heat.*

Heat emanates from the volcano—
life.

Spits you out.

>   *This bitch?*

She makes the world go round.

Everyday is a vaginal reckoning.

She's coming for you.

Eye of the hurricane.

Look at her in the spotlight.

Red door,
curtains to the world.

She put you on this stage.

Bow.

Standing ovation vagina.

PISCES: VORACIOUS APPETITE

Ryden's Girl

after Mark Ryden's painting Drips *2003*

I will bleed during commute hours,
on the buses, on the trains,
while watching movies,
over buttered popcorn
& bon bons, everything melting
together, leaking

slowly onto the floor. The soles
of my shoes will make a sticky noise
when I leave and walk down the street
picking up good men
for money, bleeding on paper
& white linen.
I'll bleed spirals

when we make love, I'll decorate
strangers.
I'll sit next to you.
Next to you.
Next to you.

& you.
I'll bleed,
cook dinner, fold laundry
blood flowing & bubbling,
bleed blossoms for fancier functions.
Arrange all my red roses
for you.

Not So Ancient Mariner

The launch of a ship involves a certain sullying,
taking her by the helm and the breaking of a bottle
over the breasts of her prow, the spume bubbling in a public
spectacle to mark her owned. The mermaid, kraken, stingray
and mollusk watch for the wave of dead albatross and swan
songs. Young men are always encouraged to travel, taught
they are destined to be gentlemen and explorers. They set off
to conquer the crustacea of your ocean floor, the mangled
root of your mangrove, the vortex of your eddy, the lichen
of your tide pools, the stars of your regeneration.
They are told it is their duty to return to land and tell tales,
but the rite of passage is hers.

Nighttime is Brackish Water

Creatures swim and slither beneath the living
when they sleep. Grandmother keeps one milky
eye open. Crocodilia circle ankles, and wet
climbs white nightdresses. Green midnight
pulses with eels and Crotalus adamanteus. We
grow gills and sweat frogs as we run barefoot
through forest. Skin is damp with anticipation of
being consumed again and again. Grandmother
opens her telescope gaze, praises mother's slender
snout. We are heavy with dorsal armor, we'll
never be able to land a man it is said. We are
saltwater, we are drowning. The clasp on the
door is a secret.

Polar

I am in search of the ice fish maw—

a cold red slit.

    An opening,

a question of expectation.

This is the thought that excites me:
Your sex
glacial—sticky, prickly as the glass worm.
That deep sea creature,
the sparkle of your inner Antarctic.
& I, bottom trawl
spongy and bat-starred, full up
with dark ribbons, am held tight
by tentacles that bite.

The crawl and squirm is a test-
ament, that I am not afraid
of your atmosphere.

So, I enter through the slush and ice.

Understand it best not to excite
about the hunt—

six months of night,
six months of light,

instead,
content,
and moor

to the peculiar thrill
of our doom, strange
genesis, a white crocodile fish and its krill

In Passing, I Mention Researching the History of Female Genitalia for Two Years

While in bed with a now dispatched lover, I say,

> *A French engineer was hired*
> *to deal with the scourge*
> *of sexually transmitted disease in Paris.*

The engineer's qualifications:

> The design of the Paris sewer system.

We're naked, in bed. He laughs and says,

> Well, it sort of makes sense,
> don't you think?

The father of the sewer system
lined up women of all backgrounds
to prove his hypothesis:

> Prostitutes are to blame.

Poor sewer maker spent three weeks in bed,
so depressed because after lifting hundreds
of skirts he found that a virgin vagina looks pretty
much the same as a well-traveled vagina.

Engineer-sewer maker could not be deterred.
He developed a new hypothesis:

       All vaginas are guilty.

A vagina is a muscle
much like a mouth,
it has so much to say.

Swamp Thing

Lessons learned early. How when you tried to play dodge ball and the ball hit you in the face, and freckle-faced Saeed Abdel had so many questions. Took you behind the school and would you let him kiss you? And would you let him go to second base? You could only think of the red and dimpled ball meeting your face, the black eyes that followed. The black eyes that followed your mother, and you held back, and did not understand second base, still. Saeed Abdel's freckles surrounded by flesh flushed pink as he insisted, *But I'm experienced.* You heard, through the vine which was a snaked swamp, a mangrove filled with serpents, that Saeed *was experienced* because he practiced touching his little cousin's breasts when they found themselves alone. *Felt her up,* he said. *She would hide under the bed,* he said. Only certain creatures survive brackish water. Saeed told everyone *first and second and even third base.* For the rest of that year there were chants in your wake. You were the last to be picked for the team. It was a well known fact that when something came at you fast, you froze. You were assemblage of saline and troubled root systems, mangle of habitat. You being woman, being girl, you pillar of salt, you became the kind of terrain that accepts whatever settles into it. Inundation of erosion. You will never be good at group sports. Alligator and cottonmouth whispers about those types of girls rustle through the fetterbush.

The End of Eros

Should I tell you?
Sweet bitter,
hours are sparrows,
hollow-boned and ethereal.

Sweet bitter,
we are undulating
under the current,
we have hardened and grown scales.

Sweet bitter,
should I tell you?
There is nothing
but silence between us.

To end
is all that we can do,
Sweet bitter,
now that we know
each other so well.

MAMMALIA: NATURAL ENEMY

Wild

There are good bears
and bad bears.

I am one of them. She-bear,
a honey and potential
man-eating mammalian.

I forage because times are hard.
I growl at all the wrong moments—
it's the occasion
of my needs and the food
in your hands.

We've all clawed at someone.

Remind me of the year
I became the unknown
visitor.

I am still learning
Eastern & Western time.

Once I was a dancing bear.

Here are my teeth.

What do you think?

Autobiography #1 (Brown Sugar)

Gold Coast slave ship bound for cotton fields

School was full of fairytales.
Villia Fritzel was the prettiest and best-prepared
princess. She alone owned the ultimate Crayola
Crayon Collection, one hundred and fifty-two
colors to choose from. Villia long blonde and blue.

Abuela said, *Stay out of the sun. You could look
baked just right—not overdone like the blacks,
not undercooked like the whites
but you're just a little too dark.*

Hear him whip the women just around midnight

There was a boy at school I liked.
He told me I had skin like dirt,
and he did too. I tried to play
but always fell. The flesh of my knees
scraped raw by the gray asphalt.
The pink meat exposed, a wound
that filled with bright blood
that overflowed and stained
white knee high socks
that never stayed up.

Tió Charlie sang along to The Rolling Stones.

Brown Sugar, how come you taste so good?
Just like a young girl should.

It was the year that the girls at school
loved Donny and Marie
and their long white teeth.
The year the girls at school loved
Michael Jackson, *A B C, It's easy as 1 2 3.*

Papi would pet mother's white skin,
and look at me.
Family joke, *Where did I come from?*

Brown Sugar, just like a black girl...

Do You Know the Huntsman?

In Lodi you can eat burgers among 314 taxidermied animals. Portrait: Lonely visits lonely. I too was once the wild hunt until a huntsman came upon me and carved me out. Once a catch. I am still, waiting among crests of cheetah pelvis and lion mane. Some of us sharpen eye or antler. Everything connected to our bodies, a potential weapon.

The Golden Ratio

Distance between the span of a wing,

clavicle, arc on which we rest.

Measure moments as speculation.

A formula, a question of:

      How many slashes make a slish?

      Exactly what makes a girl a gash?

      Beholder of hidden flaws,

      foray into lux.

      None can deny the twang

      of eight thousand nerves.

      Why all the tremble and janksy?

      Much to discuss

      between circumstance

      and circumference.

      All we are is round and round,

      search for rational perfection.

      When we fit together like questions.

The Faculties of Sense

It was a rough year for equilibrium.
Messages rubbed the open wound
of us. In an effort to explain myself
I sometimes uttered, *I am the aftermath
of war.* On an early August afternoon,
the heat and those words,
they were sticks and stones,
they were bullets. People walked
through the streets in a deep haze
as if death was not part of the equation.
When the term *random acts* was first coined
it was not meant to mate with the words *gunmetal*
and *rapid succession.* Consider the body
left on the ground for hours. The world allowed to fester.

A solitary man, so used to his podium,
reading an autopsy as art. Recall the other poet
writing about his tribe, *that poem
not being for you.* All that is not yours.

If we could gift you this . . .

Even perception is not that malleable.

Letters From an Animal

Dear ,

I am a hooded beast, uniquely hogtied. Feed me and clothe me.

Dear ,

I am thinking of reaping & sowing & cage madness.

Dear ,

I am asunder, your pet and companion. Kick me
in the deep neurosis if I begin to chase my tail.

Dear ,

Let's hang out. I'll be the one who is shackled & hoisted.

Dear ,

Why do you leave my blood steaming?

Dear ,

I liked it better when you were afraid of me.

American Chien

She pats it
like
the family dog

Treats it
like
an umbrella

Now open
Now close

Makes it do tricks

Sticks
an eyeball in it
Scares
all the customers
Eye can see you

Persona
non grata
Vagina
dentata
that
thing

down
there

Long Deep Wound

If gash were an animal

she might be a blue whale

swallowing you whole

or a shark

taking you in pieces.

In the snowy tundra

she might be a polar bear

opening you up, the hot

steam of you

rising into the ether.

Gash might be the warmth

of the Santa Ana winds

helping to float your boat.

Remember, she's the giant eye,

the grand opening,

the place where you first appeared

hungry and glimmering—

the place you once called home.

The New Story of O

I've always hated that pink is the color of woman-girl
because I fluctuate between red & black,
to be laced in a tutu for such a long time
and to get nothing in return.

If you care to know, most days
I think about sex more
than five hundred men
gathered in a great mausoleum
for the circle jerk of all time.

Unlike them,
I never fall.

With a gyration of my hips I'll say,
Let's do it again!

I take what I want.

INSECTA: SMALL ANIMALS OF SENSATION

Ode to My Pretty Thing

My woman's wolf-head
is a twin-wing-shaped quim.

A holy hollow,
causer of woe
and want.

She's a sword
sheather.

A come hither &
burrow
in my petaled
poontang.

Pudendal cleft
and reaper,
bringer
of the little death,
gasp & scream
cream dream.

Some think her
a bad habit,
a saint noir.

Some know better
the blessed fruit.

Babylon

Scarlett Johansson's breasts look like the fluffiest pillows.

Pillows sent from god or sleep train,
which both offer a better night's sleep at a price.

Earlier today I was blinded by the sheen emanating
from a young man's torso.
I wanted to thank him for sweating,
for taking off his shirt, for being so bright.

But first, let me say that I want all women
to shine at me too.

That I may view the slope of each breast.

Once, I watched a breast on a giant screen
as it slow, dripped, milk

and I knew then why they call women witch and devil.

That translucent dew indefensible.

Billow of breast, spread of hip, that smooth area
between inner thigh & pubis.

It's a different kind of butterfly.

Overture

This is the first date and I'm thinking
of the dictionary. The word fellatio
and the fact of the word fellow,
how this doesn't mean much
because fellatio and fellow
don't always go together.

This is quite the expedition.

Small talk. We're drowning
among the restaurant's periwinkle walls.

I want to lean over, say *please don't speak,*
I just want a chance to undulate.

The intervals of my breath float, midair,
like pigeons, the birds that people hate.
The man across from me
laughs, calls his pet
my pussy . . . cat, says *I'm head of the department,*
Human Communications,
specializing in men & women.

Tells you that he never liked cats
until he watched one kill a bird.
Calls the cat's bloody muzzle charming.

Talks more about blood, why a woman
could never be president.

My kookaburra awakens, cackles emerge.

Isn't it funny, he says, *I named the kitty Killer.*

Urchin Detonator Blazon, or Ode to the Clitoris

Majora-
Minora
Corpus
Cavernosa
Clam
Climbing
Up that hill
Deep
Rooted
Long-legged
Landscape
Miscella
Landica
Alluring
Love-place
Lace
Bud
In vestibule
Misunderstood
Hood
Transcendental

Bean
Pudendal
Vessel
Oyster
Not vestal
Ring, ring
Ring my bell
Desiderata
Urchin
Inviolater
What would you say
If we let you speak?

The Most Private Thing
I'm Willing to Admit

I'm disco daddy heiress.
A good time girl.

I'm bushwhacked.

Fair warning—
emotion at the access trail,
the boot grade,
the box foot—back country.

I'm coming for you.

I'm hyrdophillic. Love the rush
of your blood
when your iceberg melts.

Years have passed zero. Hungry.

Let's do this—one two three.

Don't mourn the man

you used be.

I've climbed a mountain

just to flirt with you. Could

like you now, better than ever.

A man can wear you out,

is a perfect strawberry

until he's been picked.

The Party

We went into the moment with fastidious cheer.

The invitations, handwritten, each stamp licked by our tongues.

We called everyone's attention with taut helium-filled balloons.

The streamers, garish and bold, had no hesitation, they whored
themselves in the wind.

We had gluttony.

Women in strapless gowns fattened their bellies.

We licked our greasy fingers, teased men
until they fought one another.

We kissed for revenge and spilled as we drank.

We hid nothing, had a banquet of each other, took one another
on tables, feasted to spite old hunger.

Everything was taken and sullied.

We milked the tender fruits, seedless and wilted,
they fell apart on our fingertips.

The survivors, drunken, and the flies, blind.

We scurried off in different directions.

When My Body Becomes Glass

A finger will play my edges and make me hum like
when bees basket anthers and stamen. Name me
bruised petals. See through me. See the violet of my
natural disaster, my exposed boutique. The body no
longer hides and seeks. Stripped to basic, the blood
you make surge superior, inferior. Examination of
my starfire, my bright and empty. Let this be my
autopsy—that when you touched me you made me sing.

AVES: FEATHERS AND NAKED JAWS

Ode to the News of the Day

They say that addicts are walking on broken glass on the way
to their death.

I seek justice for all the insomniac flowers. Don't let them be
lonely.

There have been times:

>   I have never felt more alone
>   than when I was surrounded
>   by your gaze.

I am writing to say that there has been:

An air strike
A ground offensive
A plane, downed
Children on buses going nowhere
having nowhere to go
A woman in Baltimore whose body was found
and the news said, *severe trauma*,
and her brother refers to her as him
because even after we emerge
from our chrysalis
people may not
see us.

We are still learning.

Somewhere, someone

is injecting botulism into their forehead.

Today it is possible to live longer,
to erase personal history
from your face,

to inject yourself away.

The word addict comes from the Latin *addico*,

which means *devoted*.

It is the devotion of the moth to the moon

that drives it to its end.

When I say devotion I mean your face, my love. I mean

I don't care
how much glass you break. I mean,
how lovely the shine
of your brokenness.

To break down is better than to break up.

If ever I believed in anything,
it is you.

On Monday Nights, We Write

for Cassandra Dallett

Suze Orman's *Money Cards*
lean toward an unopened copy
of *Rolling Stone*, while a chubby
gold maniko neko high-fives
the air.

My friend's frosted eyes sparkle
and brim. Her tears remind
me of the pool of great
ambivalence in which the man
I love, and I, dog paddle.
Always chasing each other.

I sigh often, say things like,
> *I'm sorry for the death*
> *of drugs and*
> *having no escape*
> *and where have all*
> *my words gone.*

My friend says,
> *I still love them.*

Her blonde hair fans
around her face. She sniffles,
> *I can't fuck or write*
> *when I feel*
> *like a monster.*

We sip coffee and type.

In El Cerrito the average age
of men is likely to be over sixty-five.
I recall the last words
that I said to the man
I love as I walked out the door,
> *So listen, I'm forty-five,*
> *we need to figure this out*
> *because I don't have twenty*
> *years to process.*

There are Dutch clogs
on the coffee table,
telephones, headsets,
three pens, and poems waiting
to be workshopped,
next to *Journey's Greatest Hits.*

I wonder about comebacks.

Looking down I watch my friend's pink
toes wiggle, as she says,

> *Men have done*
> *terrible things*
> *to me but I still*
> *want one.*

The room goes quiet after that,
and we write.

Fingers hit keys and in the distance
the sound of the highway
could be an ocean.

Closer still, is the sound
of a basketball hitting concrete
over and over again. The sound
of trying to get it right.

Et Cetera

Little Girl Bin Laden is what my ex-girlfriend called me
after 9/11, and before our break up.

Last night at the fashion show I met a couple
who proclaimed that they were monogamous,
which makes them the last of their kind in San Francisco.

Love is a word like a stone. I roll it around in my mouth

The word *polyamory* has always sounded to me like an affliction.
I imagine the brain unable to message the nerves, the muscles
roped and unwilling.

Once, a friend called to invite me to an orgy.
He called it a love pit, and all I could say
was, *I'm sorry, I think you've dialed the wrong number.*

There are times when my love doesn't recognize me.
He calls out Monster! and because I am poet
and pleaser I say, *Yes dear.*

On the subject of deer, I must add
that Emily may have been wrong—
sometimes the wounded deer
doesn't leap at all.

Grounded, as in bone rubbing against bone,
skin against ragged stone—
that is the feeling of commitment.

So, I muster the strength to roll that stone again,
suck on it during my stay in this desert. Shine it
with hydrochloric acid until it is pearlized.

A gem is a hard object people still like.

I Stepped on Your Feet and
You Called me Your Favorite Dancer

Everything is pivotal no matter

that the eyes see so much pointillism.

Our story is destined for facets.

I'm ready to alter the fairytale.

Perhaps we are as good as the golden spike

and maybe we were the first tenement

and the first slum

but when your mouth met mine

it was Vitruvian. We leveled the place.

We could have been a lithograph, rubbed and rubbed.

Let's be honest, we were no cliff hanger,

though we had our moments.

Pigeon Woman

They call you
misguided
and slightly foul.

You are wing-tied,
here comes birder,
watcher, and keeper.

Lifespan is wing span.
You have to spread
and work it. Remember,

heaven is a great deal
more romantic as an idea
because people lie. They will

say: your lord & savior
is living on a cumulus cloud
and you, being poet,
and you, being woman,
knew it was too late

from the start. Bad habits
wind round you as rosary
and strangulation prayer—

nest, be good, bind breast,
clip wings. Assemblage of bird—
perched feathered thing.

A cage refused. You claw
toward auspice, tough
as rock dove, pure bird
of the street.

Luminous Phenomenon

We built a butterfly shack from the blueprints of our bodies. The spreading of our wing in a pinhole, and then flight. Dirty picture, blurry picture. The distance, a bird's eye-view. Like two sticks, we might look perfectly useless to others. Together, we burned, found hidden gems, and offerings sometimes as tiny as the tongue's papilla. Incandescence emerged from the close study of faces and frames. Each new image, a nest of vulnerabilities. We explored them all. This is a song to sensation, a hail to Pacinian cells, one and all. Exposing ourselves brought a resurrection. We arose superheroes of capturing the moment, we braved the dangerous internet swamps. Oh risk, oh vicaria. The denuded body was no SOS, but a beckoning to explore the hothouse that grows beneath flesh.

Getting the Bird Out

after Kiki Smith's Getting the Bird Out 1992

There was a pinked thread that connected us. *Little bird*, I would coo, and suck gently, for fear of dismantling that delicate flesh, vernal, eternal. My mouth was the only thing that it suffered. Poor thing, and I was glad it was named *thing* because it gave us a chance—his thing and my thing—two who were both wretched.

Sometimes, I remember a boy who brought me all matter of breathing things. Once upon a time it was a frog, its sacrificial life on display, the corners of flesh pinned & pulled in opposite directions.

On the matter of size, I was instructed never to combine certain words, and I being beaked, learned the lesson swiftly as a swallow. I began to cough feathers at dinner parties. My lover blamed my upbringing, the monthly disposition. I worked hard as always, covered my mouth with hands shaped like wings, and thought of fledglings, their tiny beaks breaking the sky open when they try for the first time.

Ursa Major

When I said I wanted a wedding gown, I didn't mean
put out the stars and the afterthought *oh no, what have I done.*

I didn't mean let's invite our friends to get drunk
and drowsy and slowly disappear. Monogamy
should not be wearing a girdle, an iron lung
or a polyester pant-suit.

Wedding gown should not mean covering every mirror
in the house because our reflection has disappeared.

What I meant was lift my veil, bring sparrows
to crown my head and invite every sweet animal
in the kingdom to sing.

I didn't mean let's black-hole the aurora borealis.

It used to be that a man could take his wife
to a doctor who would slide something sharp
into her and scramble the unhappiness
right out of her brain.

When I said I wanted a wedding gown, I meant
I am a wild beast, three leaps of the gazelle.
Let me shine.

I wanted the heat that comes with the atmosphere
of our separate lives, to be stripped
of all gowns, to shine like Ursa Major.

I wanted a galaxy, the universe.

For Broken Blossom

after Joseph Cornell's Crystal Cage, *1953*

Please
recognize
yourself
I have made
memories for
you and placed
them in a box
in the heavens
Strange dove
of flotsam you are
Joan of Arc, broken blossom
please recognize yourself

I have made	memories
for Joan of Arc	broken blossom
please recognize	yourself I have
made memories for	you and placed them
in a box in the	heavens Strange
dove of flotsam	you are proof
not everything needs an	explanation or a cage

Temple of the Femina

Womanhood is no gutter.

In the city of want we find ourselves
behind every door.

It takes a certain kind of injury
to create the sacrificial lamb.

Dear Flower,

We may find ourselves
in a hothouse of writhing
body parts; a torso for art,
a liver for anger.

We are hysterical. We are floating.
Un-rooted and free.

ACKNOWLEDGMENTS

I would like to thank Nomadic Press, especially J. K. Fowler, for his vision and commitment to creating the kind of publishing house that is relevant to the world that we live in; Michaela Mullin, for the gift of her editorial prowess and incredible patience; Michelle Ruiz Keil, for believing in my writing and me, longer than any other person has—this book, and life in general, would not exist without her; all of the writers and literary powerhouses who offer inspiration and support and little bits of kindness on the most necessary days—Cassandra Dallett, Sharon Coleman, Paul Corman-Roberts, Tomas Moniz, Nick Johnson, Richard Loranger, Ajuan Mance, Tongo-Eisen-Martin, Kwan Booth, Joyce Jenkins, Maw Shein Win, Arisa White, Baruch Porras-Hernandez, Joel Landmine, Missy Church, Lauren Traetto, Norma Smith, Youssef Alaoui Fdili, Cyrus Armajani, and countless others. I would also like to thank Amanda Ayala and Araceli Ayala—for reminding me of why I must keep writing. As always, I thank Connor and Sayre, who gave me life and and the desire to make more art.

And many thanks to the editors of the following journals in which some of these poems, in some version have appeared:

Antimuse and *Lummox Press:* "San Quentin Senryu"; *Aspasiology*: "Letters From An Animal," "The Melancholy of U.S. Architecture," "Not So Ancient Mariner"; *Cherry Bleeds*: "Observations in New Orleans"; *Dogwood Review*: "The Party"; *East Bay Review*: "Et cetera;" *Eleven Eleven*: "Ode to the News of the Day" and "A Sterling

Elegy"; *Generations Literary Journal* and *Story Magazine*: "Convocation"; *Gorgon Poetics*: "Long Deep Wound" and "The End of Eros"; *Lummox Press*: "Meat Tags";Hysteria Anthology, *Lucky Bastard Press*: "Industrial Vagina" and "Flames Rise From a Woman's Breast"; *Jam Tarts Literary Magazine*: "Faculties of Sense" and "The Golden Ratio"; *Macaroni Necklace*: "Voice Culture"; *Oakland Review*: "On Monday Nights We Write"and "In Passing, I Mention Researching the History"; *Penumbra*: "Ursa Major"and "Luminous Phenomenon"; *Red Light Lit*: "With a Mouth Like That," "Ode to My Pretty Thing," and "The Eighth House"; *Rivet*: "What I Might Carry in the Small Cave of My Mouth," "How to Write a Love Letter," and "Autobiography #2" *Rusty Truck*: "I Stepped on Your Feet and You Called Me You Favorite Dancer" and "Overture"; *Sparkle & Blink*: "Artemis," "Do You Know the Huntsman," "Polar," "Wild," "Ideation," "American Chien," and "Baby—Our—Sorrow," "Broken Blossom," When My Body Becomes Glass"; *Tattoosday*: "Temple of My Femina"; *The Walrus*: "Portrait"; *Word Riot*: "Ryden's Girl"; *Zeitgeist Press*: "The New Story of O"; *Zygote in My Coffee*: "Disneyland," and "My Little Pony."

MK CHAVEZ is the award-winning author of *Mothermorphosis* and *Dear Animal,*. Chavez is co-curator of the reading series Lyrics & Dirges, co-director of the Berkeley Poetry Festival, and has been guest curator of the reading series at Berkeley Art Museum and Pacific Film Archive. She has been a visiting instructor at Stanford University, San Francisco State University, Mills College, and Hedgebrook. She is the recipient of an Alameda County Arts Leadership Award, the PEN Oakland Josephine Miles Award. Her recent publications can be found in bags of coffee from Nomadic Coffee and on the Academy of American Poets Poem-A-Day series.